COLD SPRING IN WINTER

Valérie Rouzeau
COLD SPRING IN WINTER
P A S   R E V O I R

Translated by
Susan Wicks

Introduced by Stephen Romer

2009

Published by Arc Publications,
Nanholme Mill, Shaw Wood Road
Todmorden OL14 6DA, UK

Original poems copyright © Valérie Rouzeau 2009
Translation copyright © Susan Wicks 2009
Introduction copyright © Stephen Romer 2009

Design by Tony Ward
Printed in Great Britain by the
MPG Books Group, Bodmin and King's Lynn,

978 1904614 30 2 (pbk)
978 1904614 59 3 (hbk)

ACKNOWLEDGEMENTS
Pas revoir was first published in 2003 by le dé bleu
and is reproduced by kind permission of the publishers.

Susan Wicks's translations have appeared in the following
journals: *Poetry London, Poetry Review, La Traductière* and the
Everyman edition of Apollinaire, edited by Robert Chandler.

Cover photograph: Marie-Céline Nevoux Valognes

The publishers acknowledge financial
assistance from
ACE Yorkshire

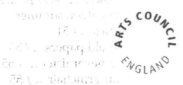

**Arc Publications: 'Visible Poets' series
Editor: Jean Boase-Beier**

CONTENTS

SERIES EDITOR'S NOTE

The *Visible Poets* series was established in 2000, and set out to challenge the view that translated poetry could or should be read without regard to the process of translation it had undergone. Since then, things have moved on. Today there is more translated poetry available and more debate on its nature, its status, and its relation to its original. We know that translated poetry is neither English poetry that has mysteriously arisen from a hidden foreign source, nor is it foreign poetry that has silently rewritten itself in English. We are more aware that translation lies at the heart of all our cultural exchange; without it, we must remain artistically and intellectually insular.

One of the aims of the series was, and still is, to enrich our poetry with the very best work that has appeared elsewhere in the world. And the poetry-reading public is now more aware than it was at the start of this century that translation cannot simply be done by anyone with two languages. The translation of poetry is a creative act, and translated poetry stands or falls on the strength of the poet-translator's art. For this reason *Visible Poets* publishes only the work of the best translators, and gives each of them space, in a Preface, to talk about the trials and pleasures of their work. From the start, *Visible Poets* books have been bilingual. Many readers will not speak the languages of the original poetry but they, too, are invited to compare the look and shape of the English poems with the originals. Those who can are encouraged to read both. Translation and original are presented side-by-side because translations do not displace the originals; they shed new light on them and are in turn themselves illuminated by the presence of their source poems. By drawing the readers' attention to the act of translation itself, it is the aim of these books to make the work of both the original poets and their translators more visible.

Jean Boase-Beier

TRANSLATOR'S PREFACE

I first met Valérie Rouzeau's work through Stephen Romer's translation of two poems from *Pas revoir* in his *Twentieth-Century French Poems*, published by Faber in 1988. Born in 1967, she is the youngest poet included in that volume. Even then I was at once attracted and intrigued by the dense word-combinations and associative leaps, as well as by the concrete autobiographical detail that seemed to set her poems apart from most other contemporary French poetry – but I was quite unprepared for the impact of the *Pas revoir* sequence as a whole. Then I met her at the 27th Festival Franco-anglais de Poésie in Paris in the summer of 2004 and, in the process of our mutual translations of each other's work, was introduced to *Pas revoir* in its entirety. Excellent as Stephen Romer's translation is, those two discrete poems he had translated were suddenly transformed by their original context into something far more vivid, emotive and poetically ambitious.

I found the whole sequence astonishing. It wasn't only the strange voice, or the obviously experimental, dislocatory techniques, but above all the powerful, intimate, even domestic underlying narrative which was somehow hugely alive on each re-reading, newly experienced in all its emotional complexity. Far from being in the service of an experiment in language for its own sake, the modernist techniques Valérie Rouzeau used answered a psychological necessity: in the tradition of great narrative modernists, they were themselves the translation of a particular emotional state. I was reminded of the Joyce of the opening of *A Portrait of the Artist as a Young Man* and of *Ulysses*, the Faulkner of *The Sound and the Fury*, where the dislocations of language seem actually to equate to implied realities of perception, as well as a gamut of other literary voices from Montaigne and Pascal through Apollinaire and Boris Vian to Sylvia Plath. The language was contemporary, slangy, playful, childlike, sometimes provocative – but it was also patently not gratuitous. It seemed to have a deep psychological justification; it wasn't destructively ironic; on the contrary, it was painfully alive and responsive and full of meanings. But the texts themselves were, from a translator's point of view, visibly difficult. The whole sequence was a translator's dream or a translator's nightmare. The first line of the first poem ('Toi mourant man au téléphone pernoctera pas voir papa.') had me blinking. The word "montre" lower down was obviously a pun – the noun "(wrist)watch" and the verb "show" – and I could have a stab at the same effect with a parallel pun in English, even if the verbal meaning of "watch" wasn't the same as the French. But "mouranrir déséspérir" weren't even words, though they had more meaning than most familiar words had. The whole poem seemed full of odd juxtapositions and inversions and puns and coinages. And yet it wasn't in the slightest academic or ignorable: the human meanings came through with a force that made me feel as if I'd been punched, leaving me gasping for breath.

I don't think I'm a born translator. The voices I can truly hear and inhabit in the way I hope I've inhabited this one are very few. And it was partly the challenge of the undertaking that attracted me. *How can I possibly…?*, I asked myself. But couldn't I just cut through my natural deference and see what happened? And mightn't 'what happened' actually feel – and be – quite close to the original? This is the task I set myself, a task quite as pleasurable and rewarding as any translation work I've ever attempted.

I was very aware, throughout, of my inadequacies. Stephen Romer had opened the way so well that I couldn't hope to do better. All I could hope to do was more – systematically and coherently to bring this extraordinary voice to an English-speaking public as closely as I possibly could. I wasn't familiar with anything like it, in French or English. Perhaps discovering Valérie Rouzeau's poems, even in my English translation, would give others something of the same feeling of exhilaration and possibility her work had triggered in me.

And certainly in terms of language itself I have learned a lot – about poetry, but also about both French and English. Since encountering the richness and ingenuity of this poetry I've learned to look at both languages slightly differently, and I don't think my response to any poetry – past or present, in English or French, my own or other poets' – can be quite the same.

We in English-speaking countries are accustomed to thinking of the French language as "poorer" than English. Most past or current Anglophone students of French are probably to some extent familiar with the history of the Académie française and its veto on new coinages. Its influence on a contemporary French language which has readily adopted foreign words while officially condemning their use can still be felt. The conventional argument is that French has gained in purity and clarity of expression what it may have lost in terms of nuance and choice. But my guess is that few of us have stopped to think about the poetic consequences of the Académie's restraint. Valérie Rouzeau's poetry makes us remember that impoverishment on one level may be an invitation to enrichment on another. Reading this poetry, you can't help feeling that French was just crying out for a poet to roll up her sleeves and get her hands dirty in exactly this compellingly human way.

For Valérie Rouzeau, the traditional purity of the French language is a kind of invitation to find something closer to the reality of lived experience. Puns, slang, hybrids, coinages, Anglicisms, baby-talk, inversions, words which seem to belong equally to the phrase that precedes them and the one that follows – it's all here. No doubt in the future scholars will sort it all into piles, as Rouzeau's father sorted his scrap metal, paper and glass. But for the moment it coheres in a language which is new-minted – rich, surprising, and yet entirely comprehensible and immediate, even childlike.

From a translation point of view, the challenge was at its most acute in poem 25, 'Le ciel se danse' (p. 48). Not only was the composite image of the first line ("standing on the pedals"; "dancing itself") impossible to translate in a single word, but the two meanings of "plateaux" in line 6 ("gear-change"; "plateaus") are simply not available in English. Here, as often in the sequence, I had to weigh up the semantic claim of the individual word against the meaning of multivalency itself. Here, as often elsewhere, I initially rejected the most obvious dictionary definition. My mind's eye saw the gears of a bike, but also hot-air balloon cows, resting on a plateau. I needed a word that was part bike and part balloon. But such a word simply didn't exist. In the end I decided reluctantly that the search had defeated me, and I'd just have to allow myself to collect a bit more junk.

The decisions were hardly ever easy. What I've tried to preserve is not only a sequence of very concrete, precise, emotive pictures of ordinary life, but also the – equally emotive – meanings of the poetic technique itself. It's a gamble. I'm reminded of how Kenichi Horie crosses the Pacific in his boat made of recycled drink-cans in poems 27 ('Vieux vieux papiers', p. 52) and 54 ('La rêve à Kenichie Horie', p. 88). Perhaps this sequence about the death of Valérie Rouzeau's father will be able to cross the Channel in a craft of recycled language in a similar way. It ought not to be a very large distance. I cross my fingers for his safe arrival. I hope he's saying *ia ora na* now, even to the smaller, plainer shells.

Susan Wicks

INTRODUCTION

In 1999 a slim collection of poems entitled *Pas revoir* came out from le dé bleu, a small publisher devoted to contemporary poetry of the type that still exists in France, producing limited print-runs of handsome books printed on good paper. But what these pages contained, in seventy-eight brief texts, was quite out of the ordinary. Here was the shock of an authentically new voice, in its urgent, stammered cadences, in which an adult, and the little girl she used to be, join together to compose a lament for her dead father. The poet who managed to intertwine these voices was a young woman in her early thirties called Valérie Rouzeau. From the opening words of her first text, the reader is plugged into a high voltage, capable of delivering jolts and shocks:

> Toi mourant man au téléphone pernoctera pas voir papa.
> Le train foncé sous la pluie dure pas mourir mon père oh steu plaît tends-moi me dépêche d'arriver.
> Pas mouranrir désespérir père infinir lever courir –
> (p. 20)

Instantly striking is the strangeness and tension in the expression, the mixed registers, the arcane word "pernoctera" coming from (so Valérie Rouzeau tells me) the verb "pernocter", ("to pass the night"), and taken from the dictionary of rare words that used to fascinate her. Next there is the colloquialism of the pleading child "oh steu-plaît tends-moi" where ambiguity hovers around "tends-moi" as in the reduced form for "wait for me" but also "stretch out" as in "'tretch out your hand to me". And then there are the neologisms, and the "mots-valises": "mouranrir", "désespérir" and "infinir", which massage, or perhaps pummel, stiff French syntax into an unaccustomed elasticity. As Susan Wicks justly says in her Translator's Preface, these words seem to be packed with meaning, and energized by their metamorphosis into verbs. It was this voice, then, that so impressed the critics, and one in particular, the influential poet and publisher André Velter, wrote in *Le Monde des Livres* of a poetry violent in its capacity to exult and disturb. He likened the whole sequence to a single breath, but the delivery is urgent, itself out of breath.

My first encounter with Valérie Rouzeau was at the University of Tours, where she was studying English. Early on, her appreciation of the pun was sharpened when she misheard in a serious lecture "key notions" as "keen oceans". After that, there was no stopping her. Her own poetry (as the examples above confirm) crackles with puns, elisions and neologisms, and delights in turning clichés inside out or on their head. But she progressed sufficiently in her English studies to undertake, for her Masters degree, a translation of Sylvia Plath's *Crossing the Water*, a formidable challenge that she carried out with passion and determination. Her engagement with the work of Plath has been continuous since then – her translation of *Ariel* is forthcoming from Gallimard, and her little monograph on the American poet (*Sylvia Plath*, Editions JeanMichelPlace, 2002) is remarkable both for its empathy and its perspicacity. It possesses also the decisiveness of one who has meditated, lived indeed, her subject: "I cannot stop myself from thinking that the energy that drives the poems of Sylvia Plath... is the same energy she had to deploy to keep herself alive, for and against everything, for and against everyone." The tone is different – Rouzeau is less corrosive than Plath – but the French poet has learned from her model much about energy and rhythm, and about "rage and refusal"; there is something of Plath's "indefatigable hoofbeat" in the syncopated, broken rhythms of *Pas revoir*.

I think, before meeting Valérie Rouzeau, I had never quite seen the legendary chameleon poet, living off words and air and (until recently) tobacco. Our first meeting outside the "grey secondary air of the university" (Plath again!) was in Tours, in a little flat overlooking a barracks, near the Botanical Gardens. With her then companion, Jean-Pascal Dubost, the place was like a monitoring station of the contemporary poetry scene. She was editing a little magazine, *La squelette laboureur*, and he *Le guide céleste*, definitely a match made in Baudelaire. There, and in succeeding lodgings, a little house in Tours the other side of the Loire, and in her current inner recess in Saint-Ouen, Valérie seems to inhabit a fragile tent of poetry books. In one of her first residences, held at the public library at Pantin, within a tough suburban circumscription of Paris, Rouzeau re-constructed what she called her "cabane", literally a kind of hideaway, made of old car seats and bits of roof and sides, recuperated from her father's scrap metal business. It was a poetry hut, a refuge, a library within a library, furnished with her personal collection of books by friends, mentors, and certain affectionately acknowledged *monstres sacrés*, (Villon, Shakespeare, Rimbaud, Apollinaire, Desnos). These days, Valérie lives by giving readings, often with musical accompaniment, and in duo with André Velter; she writes reviews, she holds workshops in schools and occupies residencies, and generally lives *une vie en poésie*, as people often remark, a rarer phenomenon still perhaps in France than it is in Britain now. It is exhausting work for her, and she is clearly loved by those who benefit from what she does. When not ministering to the poetic needs of others, she "undergoes" intense bouts of writing, and in 2002 a further substantial volume of her poetry, *Va où*, was published to critical acclaim.

The eldest of seven children, Valérie Rouzeau was born in 1967 near Nevers in the Burgundy region. When she was a little girl, her father, a dealer in scrap metal, had set down in front of her, as a Christmas present, the remains of a van, complete with seats, roof and sides, that had been hoisted up, and salvaged whole by her father's crane. This kind of experience, recollected in adulthood, is the bedrock of *Pas revoir*, and it furnishes the book's most indelible imagery. In conversation, Valérie Rouzeau uses a favourite analogy: she gathers choice fragments of language, of songs and sayings, often related to the joyous unconstrained "babil" of childhood (how a baby chants in repeated syllables, on the brink of words), just as her father sorted his metals on his truck – "le cuivre et l'alu, le zinc et l'étain" – and elsewhere, in translation, "Red brass, bronze (from grapeshot, turning) other worn-out metals...". Her father, she tells me, was given much to laughter and to tears, his "gleaming lorry" now "sleeping among the dandelions", his collection of metals now inlaid in his daughter's poems.

This brief introduction is not the place to enter into academic discussion of Rouzeau's influences, nor indeed into the particular problems her work poses for the translator. We have Susan Wicks's enlightening Translator's Preface for that. Suffice it to say that her description of *Pas revoir* as being, on first sight, either "a translator's dream or a translator's nightmare" seems apt, not least because – and this is rare – the audacity of the French inspires English, already a rich and flexible language, to new flights. Usually it is French that has to undergo the "fortifying" calisthenics, to adapt a remark of Victor Hugo's, which might enable it to absorb the radical strangeness of a Shakespeare! So this is a pleasant reversal. And I cannot end without applauding the remarkable partnership – I have it on first-hand authority that poet and translator have worked together phrase by phrase – and since Valérie Rouzeau has also translated my own poems, I know the level of commitment and scrupulousness she brings to bear on her work. The excellence, and ingenuity of these translations by Susan Wicks speak for themselves. I am especially pleased that she has continued and made good the transposition of this pure and singular voice into English.

Stephen Romer

COLD SPRING IN WINTER

Toi mourant man au téléphone pernoctera pas voir papa.

Le train foncé sous la pluie dure pas mourir mon père oh steu plaît tends-moi me dépêche d'arriver.

Pas mouranrir désespérir père infinir lever courir –

Main montre l'heure sommes à Vierzon dehors ça tombe des grêlons.

Nous nous loupons ça je l'ignore passant Vierzon que tu es mort en cet horaire.

Pas mourir steu plaît infinir jusqu'au couloir blanc d'infirmières.

Jusqu'à ton lit comme la loco poursuit vite vers Lyon la Part-Dieu.

Jusqu'à ton front c'est terminé tout le monde dans la petite chambre rien oublier.

You dying on the phone my mum he will not last the night see dad.

The train a dark rush under rain not last not die my father please oh please give me the get there soon.

Not deadying oh not desperish father everlast get up run fast –

Hand watch the time we've got to Vierzon outside it's tipping hail.

We miss each other I have no idea passing through Vierzon that in these train arrival times you've died.

Not die oh please but everlast until the nurses' corridor of white.

Until your bed as fast the engine into Lyon la Part-Dieu.

Until your forehead over now and all together in the little room and not forget.

Serrements de mains toutes bonnes civilisées.

Toi pas sonné, par couronné.

Moi dans mes plus lourds souliers que ton cœur plantée.

Les lilas là là les galets c'est vrai au fond des grands vases.

Rien qu'une alouette de vivante pour s'en aller.

Neige les yeux rouges ça leur fait mal.

Dans la danse des flocons main gourde ça chauffe un peu.

Qui va botter le derrière viser dans le dos?

C'était quand les vaches chantaient que les pies riaient.

Le monsieur de la ville vient pour tout balayer.

La neige se salit vite comme lieu commun dit-il.

Que les vaches chantaient.

Handshakes all well and civilised and good.

No bells to ring you out, no wreath.

Me in my clumpy shoes I'm heavier on earth than your deep heart.

The lilacs there and there the pebbles true inside to weight the biggest vases.

Nothing alive to leave here but a lark.

Snow when your eyes are red it hurts.

In the dance of the snowflakes hand is numb it burns a bit.

Who's going to put the boot in shoot you in the back?

When the magpies laughed the cows would play.

The gentleman from town has come to sweep it all away.

Snow soon goes black he says the same old joke.

When the cows would play.

Mon père son camion roule sur la terre, le soleil chauffe ses métaux bien triés empilés : le cuivre et l'alu, le zinc et l'étain.

De là-haut les pies n'arrêtent pas de saluer.

La grue à chenilles creuse des ornières où l'eau de pluie se trouvera belle.

L'herbe a des insectes verts qui chantent juste partout sur elle.

Et elle danse.

Ils ont shooté très fort dans les gras œillets d'Inde comme ils avaient dix ans.

Je trouve le ballon rond.

Il n'y a pas de quoi je pense trois fois car ils sont trois.

Retournent à leur anniversaire.

Moi s'ils restent ensemble j'ai leur âge mais je manque beaucoup de ballon.

Je manque d'œillets d'Inde.

My dad his lorry driving over the earth,
the sun warming his metals sorted neatly
into piles: copper and aluminium, zinc and
tin.

From high up there the magpies keep on
greeting.

The crane with caterpillar tracks is
making ruts where rainwater will like the
way it looks.

The grass is full of green insects singing
all over it in tune.

And it dances.

When they were ten they blasted their
shots at goal right in the lush french marigolds.

I find the rolling ball.

You're welcome I'm thinking three times
welcome as there's three of them.

All going birthday back.

Me if they stay together I'm their age but
really miss the ball.

Miss the french marigolds.

Parmi tout par milliers comme plumes comme casseroles où fond la neige calme de l'année qui finit.

Parmi tous les paquets déballés par toutes les fenêtres, la plainte des flaques où ne rêve pas d'étoile.

Les rubans les papiers glacés les boîtes vides ne sont plus de navires.

La neige a ses rêves qu'elle ignore de tant tomber de ciel sur nous.

C'est une proche on peut l'appeler Neige la tutoyer très vite.

Mais un salut par amen d'elle et dire Flocon à chaque fois !

Flocon tu fonds sur le cœur de mon père, Flocon tu brûles à son front...

Beau neige voix blanche.

In the middle of everything in thousands like feathers like saucepans where the snow's melting the calm snow of the year's ending.

Among all the unwrapped parcels through all the windows, the misery of starless puddles empty of dreaming.

The ribbons shiny paper empty boxes no more boats for sailing.

The snow has dreams it doesn't know about with so much falling sky on us.

She's one of us you can call her Snow no need to be polite.

But this quick hello-amen of hers and saying Flake each time!

Flake you're melting on my father's heart, Flake you're burning on his forehead...

Beautiful snow white-out voice.

Ce n'est pas quand nous cessons de parler ni même toi qui ne dis plus rien ton silence.

Ce n'est pas tous les trains partis les mouchoirs tout blancs sur les quais.

Plutôt ce qui les fait valser.

L'air jamais joué jamais stoppé.

Maintenant les clairons les violons sont à toi.

Et les mouchoirs tout blancs comme s'ils savaient des bouts d'éternité.

Des morceaux de musique.

It isn't when we stop talking nor even your not saying anything any more your silence.

It isn't all the trains that have left the brilliant whiteness of the hankies on the station platform.

It's what makes them dance a waltz.

The tune that's never played and never broken off.

Now the clarions and violins are yours.

The hankies too all white as if they knew little bits of eternity.

Pieces of music.

Une fourmi à ma chaussure je la regarde comme elle danse sur le lacet sans avoir peur.

Elle sera tombée d'herbes folles ou de mon bouquet de coucous qui lourdit mesure que j'avance.

Je quitte la pompe et je la souffle elle a une si petite vie noire.

Elle m'aurait chatouillé les pieds peut-être fait rire toute seule sur la route du cimetière comme si c'était moi comme si c'était elle.

Là plantée ni bronchante ni pensante ni rien.

Et de la façon sûre des arbres et définitive en chêne.

Comme rien comme personne ta vie.

Mal mouchée dans des mouchoirs d'au revoir de rêve, soufflée d'un coup.

Du vent, des clous.

An ant on my shoe I watch it how it dances on the lace without a trace of fear.

It must have fallen out of the long grass or from my bunch of cowslips heavier the more I walk.

I take my shoe off blow the ant away such a small black life.

It might have tickled my feet maybe made me laugh all by myself on the cemetery road as if it were me as if it were itself.

Stuck there in the ground not flinching or thinking or anything.

And in the certain, final way of trees and made of oak.

Like nothing nobody your life.

Snot-nosed in the goodbye hankies of my dreams, suddenly put out.

Wind, nails.

Les roses peuvent bien rougir dans les plus vieux jardins elles ne sont pas le cœur sorti de la mémoire.

Énormes palissades et ça monte à la tête en couronnes de rien.

Là où les jeux nouveaux étaient juchés facile l'éternité valdingue.

Ça tombe un peu beaucoup le derrière et les joues.

Et mon père là-dedans grondant ou se marrant mon père qui a trente ans peut-être et tout le temps.

Rien à mettre pour aller avec les yeux rouges.

Les lapins blancs ont beau être inno-cents tu ne dis plus d'histoires.

Et mes bouquets se cassent en deux le vent me lève ma seule robe bleue pour l'emporter au paradis.

C'est un regard dur à porter.

Toujours courir.

The roses may well go red in the oldest gardens they're not the heart out of memory.

Gigantic stockades where it goes to your head in crowns of nothing.

Where the new toys balanced easy eternity falls flat on its face.

Falling a bit a lot behind and cheeks.

And my father in all that grumbling or having a laugh my father thirty years old perhaps and all the time in the world.

Nothing to wear to go with red eyes.

White rabbits can be innocent as anything you don't tell stories any more.

And my bunches of flowers break in half the wind blows up my one blue dress to take it up to heaven.

A hard look to sustain.

Always running.

Nous n'irons plus aux champignons
le brouillard a tout mangé les chèvres
blanches et nos paniers.

Nous n'irons pas non plus dans les
cités énormes qui sont des baleines
grises très bien organisées où nos cœurs
se perdraient.

Ni au cinéma ni au cirque, ni au café-
concert ni aux courses cyclistes.

Nous n'irons pas nous n'irons plus
pas plus que nous n'irons que nous ne
rirons pas que nous ne rirons plus que
nous ne rirons ronds.

We won't go mushrooming again the fog has swallowed everything the white goats and our baskets.

We won't be going to the enormous cities either which are highly organised grey whales our hearts would soon get lost.

Nor to the cinema or circus, the *café-concerts*, the cycle races.

We won't go we'll not be going any more no more than we won't go than we won't laugh we won't be laughing any more than we won't break up laughing.

Le hangar sa tôle ondule avec du vent.

En bottes c'est à mon père il y a ses traces de doigts sur les pinces coupantes et les nids d'hirondelles.

Dogue et moi parmi les flaques sombres les grues au sommeil lourd – c'est ce qu'elles lèvent.

Robe noire le cœur le cambouis bien cachés.

Ta gueule dogue ta gueule dogue le jour va se coucher.

Mon père aux jeux télévisés sa tête sur l'oreiller infiniment brodé.

Voir du monde.

Cinéma de plages blanches de ciels de luxe – il n'irait jamais.

Aimer bien des gens de partout.

Des bêtes, des fleurs beaucoup

The shed its iron corrugating with the wind.

Wearing boots my father's and his fingerprints on wirecutters and swallows' nests.

Me and dog between the murky puddles cranes their heavy sleep – that's what they lift.

Black dress black heart black oil well out of sight.

Oh shut up dog oh shut up dog the day is going down.

My father and the game-shows on TV his head on the pillow endlessly embroidered.

See some people.

Films of white beaches skies and luxury – he'd never go.

Liking people from all over.

Animals and flowers lots.

De dans la chambre où j'ai grandi le
gel a gelé l'eau de source.

Je dors là, craque le plastique – dehors
toute une éternité hulotte chante clair.

Avant le coucher mon père et moi
chacun à un lavabo lui se trouvant jaune
moi mentant que pas tellement.

Mais il était jonquille, forsythia, du
tout la bonne heure de printemps.

Les beaux jours vivement (qu'il disait)
vivement.

Papa dire papa dear dada pire: tu te
souviens de mon petit cheval ?

Comme ça tournait autour de la table
à roulettes de cuisine sa crinière nos che-
veux noirs au vent.

Comme ça valsait les boîtes à thé les cas-
seroles belles comme ça y allait à
dada rire oh papa rear à tout casser pas
dire?

With in the room where I grew up the freeze has frozen the bottled water.

I sleep there, crackle plastic – and outside a whole tawny eternity clear-crowing.

Before we went to bed my father me each at a basin saying he looked yellow and I lied not really.

But he was daffodil, forsythia not at all that's wonderful it's spring.

The lovely days roll on (he said) roll on.

Tell me, daddy dear, dadarling, daddy poorling: do you remember my little horse?

How it went round the table on its little kitchen wheels its mane our black hair streaming in the wind.

How the tins of tea the saucepans danced so fine as how we went for it to dada laughing daddy rear until it all breaks up not say no getting away.

Je ne porte pas spécialement d'habits noirs parce que tu n'es plus visible.

Je peux penser à toi en bleu des jours entiers.

Te trouver des fleurs qui sortent de l'ordinaire des vases assez beaux assez lourds.

C'est difficile de t'offrir quelque chose, ç'a toujours été.

L'autre fois j'ai mis mes deux pieds dans tes grandes bottes vides et ton chien est venu avec moi.

Il pleuvait et je nageais dedans, tu avais dû garder les cailloux dans tes poches.

Et l'autre fois encore je ne t'ai pas porté spécialement de bouquet.

I don't wear specially black clothes because you are no longer to be seen.

I can spend whole days thinking of you in blue.

Find you unusual flowers nice enough vases that are heavy enough.

You're difficult to buy a present for, you always were.

The other time I put my feet inside your two great empty boots and your dog came with me.

It rained and I was slopping about inside, you must have kept the stones in your pockets.

And that other time as well I didn't bring you specially a bouquet.

Parmi la dînette en morceaux de petite sœur julie.

Vols d'oiseaux ne diront jamais au revoir mais peut-être bonjour mais sûrement adieu.

Là les doigts dans les débris de vaisselle pour jouer les yeux au ciel.

Elle veut être appelée dédèle.

Ses poupées, leur sème des bouts de vrais gâteaux des restes d'éclairs qu'elles grandissent.

Encore un peu d'éternité.

Une cuillère pour papa dédé.

Among my little sister julie's broken dinner-service.

Flight of birds will never say I'll see you maybe a hello but definitely goodbye.

There with fingers in the broken fragments playing looking at the sky.

She wants to be called dédèle.

Her dolls, she sprinkles crumbs from proper cakes leftover bits of eclair to make them grow.

Another little piece of eternity.

A spoon for daddy dédé.

«C'est une colle» a dit le chirurgien
que la bile dans son corps.

Tout le sang poison à cause de la bile
qui poisse maintenant laratélefoie – une
colle a-t-il dit.

Six à huit semaines et c'est très beau-
coup pas mort pas croyable déjà déjà.

Une fois sur cent mille mais ça ne par-
donne pas – une foie sur sang bile bê ça
de rate pas qu'il a expliqué que ma mère
m'a dit même temps qu'elle pleurait
debout dans le soir même temps qu'elle
pleurait ses yeux coulaient noir.

Un drap blanc, pas un ciel déchiré.

Les oiseaux tous que j'aime arrêtés.

La chambre pleine de mouchoirs
coton, papier.

Pas un arbre plus dur.

Regards qui se posent et qui fuient.

'It's a sticky one' the surgeon said the bile inside his body.

All the blood poison from the clogging bile has now ruinedhisliver – sticky he said.

Six to eight weeks that's a long long time and not yet dead it's amazing to have come so far so far.

One in a hundred thousand but it's unforgiving – wud id a hudred bilion it's undfailig as he explained my mother told me while she cried in the evening standing while she cried her eyes were running black.

A white flag, not a torn sky.

The birds I love all stopped.

The bedroom full of hankies, cotton, paper.

No tree harder.

Eyes that look and look away.

Miroir dis-moi voir c'est ma tête?

N'ai-je pas une grimace, une nouvelle ligne aussi à me barrer le front ?

Fais voir un peu ma figure: la figure orpheline ressemblante.

Renvoie-moi tout craché mon visage si je bouge vivante.

Si je bouge encore plus tu ne vois plus du tout ma gueule de fille frappante.

J'enlève mon visage de vivante, miroir.

Pas revoir.

Tartines beurrées et gelées de groseilles j'avale.

Printemps froid c'est l'hiver encore.

Mon père son visage jaune sans bouton d'or ne mange rien ni ne regrette.

Ma mère son visage rouge itout dit-elle il ne dit pas itoute.

Mais il la chérit toute sa main dessus son cœur pas semblant de dormir semblant d'être sans rire.

Mirror just let me see is this my head?

But aren't I grimacing, a new line too a bar across my forehead?

Let me just see my face: the orphan-looking face.

Spit me my spitting image if I live and move.

If I move even more you can't even see the striking girl I was.

Mirror, I'm taking away my living woman's face.

Not see it again.

Butter-frosted currant-jelly-glazed slices of bread I swallow.

Cold spring still in winter.

My father yellow face without a buttercup eats nothing nor regrets.

My mum red-faced says dearest he doesn't say dearestess.

But he holds all of her dear his hand on heart not pretending to sleep just pretending to be not joking.

Te parler papa j'ai pu te paparler un peu un petit peu paparce que nous n'avions plus tout le temps.

Dehors le monde ses oiseaux blancs comme des avions, le mur du son.

Tes mains sur le drap blanc jaunissaient jaunissaient.

Ils n'ont sûrement pas le droit de voler aussi bas pas pas le droit de voler aussi bas tu disais.

Même même le blanc de tes yeux était jaune nous alors nous sommes tout pardonné.

Le ciel se danse.

Parfois le soleil juste en face.

Je prends son vélo à mon père.

En vitesse rayonnant comme libre.

Cadre d'alu, vaches légères.

Plateaux pour leurs panses montgolfières.

Toujours librement des rayons.

Talk to you dad I managed a bit of daddychat a chitter 'cause we didn't have that much time.

Outside the world its birds as white as planes, the barrier of sound.

Your hands on the white sheet were growing yellow yellow.

Surely they have no right to fly so low no right no fly so low you said.

Even the whites of your eyes were even yellow so we two forgave each other everything.

The sky's up on its pedals, dancing.
Sometimes the sun right in your eyes.
I take my father's bike.
Radiant with spokes as if set free.
Aluminium frame, the cows take off.
Change up on the flat for their hot-air bellies.
Always spoking freely.

Les pommes d'or en été roulées dans ton camion.

Cabine mirador au soleil qui écrase.

Pépites sur le goudron bulles qui pètent en rond.

Les pommes d'or terminées balancées à la route.

Golden jusqu'au trognon.

The golden summer apples rolled into your truck.

Your cab a lookout in the blistering sun.

Chips on the tarmac bubbles bursting in a ring.

It's over the golden apples chucked out onto the road.

Delicious to the core.

Vieux vieux papiers qu'aussi César a compressés, cartons ondulés, listings, bouquins mêlés avec journaux...

Ou bouchonnés d'imprimerie, sacs tout venant (les prix varient)?

Nickel de Severonickel, chute libre de l'inox en avril.

L'installation Myosotis de l'usine d'Isbergues d'Ugines fleur bleue sûrement pas: coulée de feuilles minces en acier inoxydable voilà.

Compliqué comme une reunion de la commission «broyeurs» du syndicat national des ferrailles.

Une barque en boîtes boisson recyclées pour traverser le Pacifique.

Calcin ménager, verre cassé.

Aluminium encore (pur, casseroles), plume d'oie blanche, demi-blanche, plomb batteries entières vides.

Cuivre rouge, bronze (mitraille, tournure) et autres métaux tous usés.

Pages de «La Récupération» que mon père lisait avec soin et emballait quand elles dataient.

Old old papers that César too has crushed,
directories and corrugated cardboard, books
and newsprint all together...

Or printers' blocks of crushed paper,
ordinary bags (prices vary)?

Nickel from Severonickel, free-fall
stainless steel in April.

Forget-me-not fittings from the Ugines
Isbergues plant blue flower absolutely not:
an avalanche of stainless leaf-thin sheets,
that's all.

Complicated as a meeting of the
'grinders'' group of the national iron-
workers' union.

A boat out of recycled drink-cans to cross
the Pacific in.

Household ashes, broken glass.

More aluminium (pure, from saucepans),
goose-feathers, white, half-white, lead
whole empty batteries.

Red brass, bronze (from grapeshot,
turning) other worn-out metals.

Pages from *The Scrap Merchant* that my
father would read with care and tie in
bundles as they dated.

Tu n'écoutes plus rien si je parle plus bas.

Ni tu n'entends plus rien des guêpes qui s'occupent de piquer les lilas.

Ni n'en vois la couleur ni celles que j'ai sur moi.

Ces bottes sont faites pour marcher tu ne chantes plus ça.

C'est de la haute fidélité ton silence m'arrête là.

Ton fauteuil pèse autant qu'il peut son poids de chose lourde et noire.

Appuie par terre son gros derrière son cœur aussi bien.

D'être là vide que veille ton chien.

A tendre les bras deux fois vains où tu ne t'essuies plus les joues.

Quand on entre il est dans son coin il s'assombrit encore.

Crapaud il exploserait dans l'eau trouble des flaques que le chien va lécher.

Quand on sort il n'a pas bougé.

You never listen to anything any more if I talk more quietly.

Nor hear a thing now of the wasps that are busy stinging the lilac.

Nor see what colour nor the ones I have on me.

These boots are made for walking you don't sing that any more.

It's high fidelity your silence stops me there.

Your armchair weighs its black and heavy object weight as heavy as it can.

Squats with its fat behind against the earth could say its heart.

Just being empty there watched over by your dog.

Stretching out its two times useless arms where you no longer mop your cheeks.

When we go in it's in its corner getting even darker.

Toad it could explode in the muddy water of the puddles that the dog's about to lap.

When we go out it hasn't moved.

Ça va quand on demande moi je dis
bien surtout s'il y a du monde je prends
sur moi très bien.

On ne me voit pas chez l'épicière san-
gloter sur les pommes de terre.

Ni aux guichets de la poste retarder
l'envoi pressé d'un colissime.

Ça va je dis sans dire et la tête et la
tête.

Ça rime à rien ta mort intérieurement
pauvre chant.

De timbres je voudrais et de patates
un carnet s'il vous plaît, un filet.

Merci beaucoup de monde.

Okay when people ask I tell them fine
especially when there are people round me
yes I'm coping fine.

You don't see me in the grocer's weeping
over the potatoes.

Nor waiting at the PO window when a
portant package has to be packed off.

I'm fine it goes I say without saying my
head my head.

It makes no sense your dying inwardly
poor song.

Some stamps I need and some potatoes
please a book, a bag.

Thanks a bundle.

Ça fait deux facile mon père et moi facile.

Je compte sur lui pour tomber d'accord avec moi.

Des nuages nous passent au-dessus, des crapauds chantent au loin leur chant bien plus beau qu'eux.

Mon père ne dit mot nous sommes tous les deux mais je suis la seule à avoir le vent dans les cheveux et lui est le seul à ne pas ouvrir les yeux.

Et je lui montre du doigt d'où vient le chant gonflé vachement des crapauds mais il connaît la fable.

Des nuages nous passent au-dessus le temps, à moi surtout qui les compte tant.

Mon père ne dit rien nous sommes différents mon père et moi là sommes deux en plan.

And that makes two it's easy dad and me it's easy.

I count on him to make my peace with me.

Clouds go over us, toads croaking in the distance singing much more sweetly than they are.

My dad doesn't say a word the two of us are here but I'm the only one to have the wind blow through my hair and he's the only one not opening his eyes.

And I show him with my finger where the really puffed up song comes from of toads but he's familiar with the fable.

Clouds go over us our time, especially for me because I count them so.

My dad doesn't say a word we're different my dad and me and both of us left stranded.

M'endors seule avec le bruit d'une abeille comme blessée de s'être approchée des lampes.

L'entends dans les livres et le bois craquer ses deux ailes d'or mais quand je rallume ne la trouve pas.

Tant pis me rendors tant pis qu'elle soit une ou mille j'ai sommeil seule avec son bruit d'une autre mortelle.

De la cabine du camion noir tu éprouvais les routes sans fin.

Et passant les vitesses la main le front dorés sûrement tu rêvais.

Quelquefois écrasais une poule sotte et blanche et ça te chagrinait.

Tu préférais l'été qui raccourcit les nuits tu avais des soucis à semer sur les routes ça faisait à ton front des lignes d'horizon.

Dans tes mains quelquefois une volaille morte qu'on ne voyait jamais.

Doze off alone with the sound of a bee that might have hurt itself by flying close to lamps.

Hear it in the books the cracking wood its two gold wings but when I flick the switch it isn't there.

Too bad I go to sleep again too bad a single bee or a thousand sleepy on my own with the noise it makes, the noise of another creature that is going to die.

From the cab of the black lorry you'd try out the endless roads.

And going through the gears your hand your forehead painted gold you surely used to dream.

Sometimes you'd run a daft white chicken over and it made you sad.

You preferred the summer with its shorter nights you sowed your cares behind you on the roads it made horizon lines across your forehead.

Sometimes in your hands a lifeless bird we never saw.

Papa ça va pas dis comme ça va plus comme ça va pas plus.

Rien qui va sans dire.

Ça va pas sans dire je vais pas comme toi ça va pas papa.

Ça va pas la tête ça va pas le foie ça va pas comme ça.

La tête alouette ça gaze gazouille pas et le cœur des fois hoquette papa.

C'est mal élevé si je mets les pieds il faudrait des ailes ça pourrait aller.

Tu me fais marcher.

Dans le journal on a parlé de ta disparition.

Il y avait ta photo mais pas de récompense.

S'ils avaient raison tous, que tu serais parti savoir où.

Moi je te verrais bien dans le Pacifique Sud disant ia ora na souriant à tout le monde et même aux coquillages plus petits ou moins beaux.

Daddy how goes it tell me no it doesn't any more like this it doesn't go no more.

Nothing which goes without saying.

It doesn't go without saying I don't go like you daddy it doesn't go.

The head won't go the liver doesn't go it doesn't go like this.

My bird-brain twitter twitters itself out and sometimes my heart hiccups daddy.

It's rude if I put my feet I need a pair of wings it could go well.

You're taking me for a ride.

In the paper they talked about your disappearance.

There was your photo but there wasn't a reward.

If they'd all got it right, that you'd gone off to find out where.

Me, I could see you in the South Pacific saying ia ora na and smiling at all and sundry even the smaller plainer shells.

Le temps toqué coucou juré à la casse où poisse le cambouis.

Toute seule un sale moment tes marteaux mon père manquent.

Tes bon dieu de marteaux frappés, coup double grâce de l'écho cogné et merde parfois sur les doigts.

Où mon père, derrière le nuage au-dessus de la grue qui monte haut des charges à construire un gratte-ciel ?

Où, dans le murmure des arbres et des gens passant sous les arbres et recevant parfois sur la main une goutte d'eau?

Où, sur le toit de la maison avec les tourterelles et la poupée chiffon irrattrapable?

Où, à la balançoire qui se balance toute seule en frôlant le chiendent ?

Ou c'est tout ouh trop haut dans ton état ouh ouh mon père ?

Time crazy cuckoo sworn to scrap where the grease sticks.

All on my own for a filthy moment your hammers are missing father.

Your good god hammers hammered double trouble blessing of the echo hit and shit sometimes your fingers.

Where my father where behind the cloud above the crane that's lifting loads up high to build a high-rise building?

Where inside the murmur of the trees and people passing under trees who feel a drop of water sometimes falling on their hands?

Where on the roof of the house with the turtle doves and the rag doll that's hopelessly lost?

Where on the swing that's swinging all on its own just brushing the weeds?

Or it's all oh where too high up there my father as you are were were?

Le ciel tout bleu sur ta tête les oiseaux bleus qui s'y jettent.

On ne les voit pas.

Je n'ai pas de fleurs sur moi là.

Ni je n'embrasse pas la route mais à pied le cœur compte bien double ?

Et sur les mains ?

Les fleurs seront bientôt très bleues.

Mon œil, tes yeux.

Ma mère rougit comme une rose pour couper tant de tartines.

J'ai mes collants filés des tout neufs sourit-elle ça fait suer.

La boulangère l'a remarqué.

C'est une grosse dame au tablier farine qui s'attarde à des riens.

Ma mère a dit en plus poli qu'elle s'occupe de son pain.

Rit et pleure en même temps qu'elle raconte les collants.

Du coup elle est rentrée directement sans passer par le cimetière.

The sky all blue on your head the blue
birds rushing there.

They can't be seen.

I haven't any flowers on me here.

Nor do I kiss the road but doesn't a heart
on foot count twice?

And what about on hand?

Soon the flowers will be very blue.

My eye, your eyes.

My mother blushes like a rose to cut so
many slices.

I've got my laddered tights on brand new
ones she tells me with a smile it drives you
mad.

The woman in the baker's noticed.

She's a fat lady with a floury apron
wasting time on trifles.

My mother said in nicer terms she knows
which side her bread is buttered.

Crying and laughing at the same time as
she tells me about her tights.

So she went straight home without
calling in to see him in his grave.

Gerbes gerbes les mêmes qu'autant de courses gagnées mon père fleuri de la tête aux pieds.

Mon père fleuri de tout ton long je suis là m'excuse de fumer mais j'aurai bientôt terminé.

Me reste juste trois malheureuses tiges, je souffle d'arroser tes bouquets et j'y vais.

Ce n'est toujours pas toi ce cadavre comme si toi tu aurais tenu en place comme ça comme si tu ne savais plus dire bonjour toi si courtois.

Et si gracieux mon père qu'on te reconnaît au sourire.

Ce n'est toujours pas toi ce visité qui n'offre rien à boire ne dit pas de s'asseoir toi si civil hospitalier pas toi c'est trop mal imité.

Sprays of flowers sprays the same so many races won my father flowering from head to toe.

My father flowered all along his length I'm there I'm sorry to be smoking but I'll have finished soon.

Just three pathetic twigs of ciggies left I'm breathless watering your bunches and I'll go.

It's still not you this corpse as if you could have just stayed put like that as if you couldn't bring yourself to say hello you always so polite.

And such a gracious man my father that we recognise you by your smile.

It's still not you this man we go to visit doesn't offer us a drink and doesn't say sit down you so polite hospitable not you they haven't captured you at all.

La robe en Jean bleue de travail et les chaussures de neige en mai.

Au bord de l'eau le temps je l'ai je l'ai tout devant moi qui coule.

En moins de deux la robe est blanche jusqu'aux chaussures et fond dans l'air.

En moins de deux la robe est bleue jusqu'à mes yeux.

Feu l'hiver feu.

Blue denim working dress and snowboots on in May.

Beside the water I have time I have it all before me flowing.

In a trice the dress is white right down to the boots and melts in the air.

In a trice the dress is blue right up to my eyes.

Fire of winter deceased.

Froid le ciment froid coulé en trois dalles égales.

Trois comme infirmières pâles disant « Vous ne savez pas ? Monsieur Rouzeau est...»

On avait traversé des prairies pluvieuses croassantes vite venir te saluer «...décédé...» toi c'est Dédé ton nom d'ami de paternel papa Dédé.

Les trois syllabes dans le désordre des infirmières toutes en chœur et bouleversées que c'est Dédé lui si gentiment si malade.

«Mais il ne s'est pas vu partir il dormait – bercé par la pluie il s'est endormi – a mouri...»

Cold the cement poured cold into three equal slabs.

Three like pale nurses saying, 'Don't you know? Mr Rouzeau is…?'

We'd crossed the rainy croaking fields of grass to quickly come and greet you 'passed away…' you that is Dédé with your friendly name of fatherly daddy Dédé.

Three syllables in chaos nurses all in chorus stunned that Dédé's dead and him so kind so ill.

'But he didn't feel himself go off he was asleep – rocked by the rain he went to sleep – he past away.'

Arrive un air de mémoire longue.

Ma grand-mère a ses cheveux noirs, un polichinelle dans le tiroir.

Peut-être aux lèvres son sourire comme une chanson qui va vieillir.

Elle rêve au ciel elle rêve aux anges tout en déroulant ses pelotes.

C'est l'hiver et la guerre est longue.

Ma mère prend la photo et puis elle a vingt ans.

On ne voit pas la voiture verte pour aller partout.

Toujours sourire ils traversent le petit pré ils voient les premières fleurs.

Ils ont un enfant chacun dans les bras les mots qu'ils aiment se disent deux fois: soleil soleil sur l'herbe sur l'herbe tu danses-tu ?

Here comes a tune with a long memory.

My grandmother's got her black hair, a bun in the oven.

Perhaps on her lips that smile of hers like a song which will soon get old.

She's dreaming of sky she's dreaming of angels as she unwinds her wool.

It's winter and the war goes on and on.

My mother takes the photo then she's twenty.

You can't see the green runabout to run about in.

Always a smile they cross the little field they see the first flowers come.

They each have a child in their arms the words they love get said twice over: sunshine sunshine on the grass the grass do you dance you dance?

Je monte l'eau là-haut l'eau calme minérale.

Pas de celle que j'ai bue en mangeant toute seule froid.

Là-haut vais me coucher après voir des étoiles.

Je sais qu'elles brillent aussi sur toi.

Des étoiles attendues en mâchant un plat froid.

Le cœur trop salé d'une bête comme repas.

I take the water up the mineral water, calm.

Not the one I drank while eating a cold supper on my own.

Up there I'm going to go to bed when I've seen the stars.

I know they shine on you as well.

Stars I've waited for while chewing on cold food.

The salty heart of an animal to eat.

Mon père avait sa maison phénix et quatre enfants donc juste assez de mains avec celles de ma mère.

Du toit nouveau le nuage rêvé se gorgeait de joie brute à redoubler d'efforts: pa bis man bis cuit bis et pépites aux volailles plus ou moins bien perchées.

Ensuite on grandirait on saurait parononcer et cul pas bis deviendrait mal élevé, amour toujours et cœur moins familier.

Mais là du toit nouveau le rêve déménageait, on comptait nos parents nos poules et tout y était.

My father had his phoenix house four children and so just enough hands together with my mother's.

From the new roof the dreamed-up cloud would swell with untamed joy to make him try still harder: dada mummy biccy crumbs for the chickens more or less clucking.

Then we'd grow up we'd know how to say the words and arse don't let me hear you say that word again not well brought up, and always love and heart not so familiar.

But there from that new roof the dream was moving on, we'd count our parents chickens everything was there.

Savoir ça voir rien à voir ça n'a et pourtant non c'est toi ta belle tête dure.

Ç'a voir avec toi quand même mais de loin toi-même n'en voyant rien de rien.

Roulé qu'on te donne des baisers dans la pièce froide sans ciel du tout, roulé j'attends j'entends qu'on t'a – papa si près je brûle je sais attends qu'on ouvre mais quelle planque.

Qu'on ouvre mais quelle planque ça y est sans ciel du tout tu fermes bien les yeux et bouh.

Toi pendant ta balade main donnée à maman chèvres belles au loin toi malade.

Toi sur ta terre natale à très petits pas qui font tout drôle.

Toi ta petite voix que couvre celle des chèvres en balaaade toi malaaade disant à maman mots secrets mots infimes de tendresse grande et comme elle belle.

Knowing no wing nothing to do with any thing but no it is still you your good hard head.

It is to do with you in spite of everything but from a distance you yourself not seeing anything of it at all.

We've got one over on you giving you kisses in the ice-cold room without a sky, we've got one over and I wait I hear they – daddy so near I'm burning knowing wait till they open it up but what a hiding-place.

Open it up but what a hiding-place that's it no sky at all you've got your eyes tight shut and boo.

You on your walk your hand in Mum's and goats in the distance beautiful, you feeling bad.

You on your native soil in little tiny steps that look quite weird.

You your little voice which drowns the goats' as walking baaack you feeling baaad saying secret tiny words of tenderness to Mum great tenderness and beautiful like her.

Il y a des échelles: on ne les touche pas.

Loin d'une fleur par battement que j'aurais voulu.

Si j'entends appeler mon nom ce n'est pas toi.

Ni moi – j'ai le cœur dans les pieds, la tête.

Du sol au soleil ce bouquet d'en rêve monte comme un record.

Scales of things are like ladders: you mustn't touch.

Far from the flower for every beat I would have liked.

If I hear my name being called it isn't you.

Nor me – my heart's in my feet, my head.

From the ground to the sun this dream bouquet is rising, beating all records.

Mon père mon père mon père en terre au vent d'été au vent d'hiver.

Oh mon père terra terraqué je te répète perroquet mon père mon père.

Au vent d'hiver au vent d'été en terre entier au vent chanté.

Enfant dans les grands sapins verts c'était toi qui sifflais soufflais enfant dans les grands sapins blancs.

Mon père je te répète en l'air c'est une fleur lancée assez haut.

Les deux pieds dans tes graviers clairs.

Les mains pour la fleur ou l'oiseau.

My father my father my father on earth as he is in summer wind in winter wind.

Oh my father in earth as he is in never I parrot it back my father my father.

In winter in summer wind all over the earth in the wind of singing.

Child in the great green pines it was you who were whistling blowing child in the great white pines.

My father I tell you again in passing I'm chucking this flower high enough.

My two feet in your light-coloured gravel.

My hands for the flower or the bird.

Ils font leur bruit de manger les voisins en petite famille.

À leur table je prendrais du chou, du chou et puis des roses et je remercierais.

La vieille sensation de dire paa la bouche pleine de midi les mains pas bien lavées mes voisins de sept ans je les envie même engueulés pour ça.

Moi paa se laisse pousser les ongles et les cheveux et ne déjeune plus et ne répond plus de rien.

Sur le toit de l'hospice au-dessus de nos têtes un homme siffle turc et bosse, mon amant de saint jean qu'il dans l'air échafaude.

Ça monte-t-il jusqu'à toi comme un trait lumineux aperçu de toi seul ?

Toi qui as toute ta vie si sifflé durement turbiné et quelquefois pleuré tout ensemble mon père.

They make their family eating noise the neighbours when they're on their own.

If I ate with them I'd have cabbage, cabbage and roses and I'd say thankyou nicely.

The way we used to feel saying Daa no not with your mouth full at dinner-time you haven't washed your hands my seven-year-old neighbours how I envy them even when they get it in the neck for that.

Not me my daa lets his nails grow long his hair and doesn't eat his dinner any more and doesn't speak for anything ever again.

On the nursing-home roof above our heads a man is whistling Turkish slogging away, my midsummer lover he scaffolds in the air.

Does it reach up to you like a shaft of light that only you've caught sight of?

You so whistling all your life and working your guts out sometimes crying all at once my father.

Le rêve à Kenichie Horie de traverser
le Pacifique sur une barque en alumi-
nium...

Tu avais dû lire cet article et sûrement
dans la cuisine ou le jardin raconter
itoute seize mille kilomètres !

La page a des mots que tu as dits
d'imprimés sous mes yeux comme
d'entendre ta voix.

Et tu expliques qu'un seul panneau
solaire alimente le moteur, les lampes et
le petit frigo et aussi la radio de Kenichie
Horie en énergie électrique lumineuse.

The dream Kenichi Horie had of crossing
the Pacific in an aluminium boat...

You must have read that article and
surely in the kitchen or the garden told her
sweetheart all of ten thousand miles!

The page has words you said printed
before my eyes like hearing your voice.

And you explain a single solar panel
powers the motor, lamps, the little fridge as
well as Kenichi Horie's radio with the
electric energy of light.

Pleut sur les fleurs par-dessus toi il pleut papa.

Plein mon sac c'est de l'eau qui tombe plein les oreilles.

Le bruit que ça fait: celui de l'éléphant pissant infiniment si tu te souviens.

On dirait que les graviers rouspètent les uns après les autres, à moins que ça soit d'être arrosés comme ça.

Suis la seule visiblement là entre les bégonias et les je sais pas quoi.

Une malheureuse averse oh rien de bien énorme.

Une dispute de graviers sans aucune mémoire.

Raining on the flowers on top of you it's raining daddy.

Filling my bag it's water falling filling my ears.

The noise it makes: the noise of an elephant endlessly peeing if you remember.

You'd think the gravel chips were grumbling at one another, unless it's because they're being watered like that.

I'm the only one visibly here among the begonias and the I don't know what.

A miserable shower oh nothing to write home about.

A feud between gravel chips raked smooth.

Suis debout dans ta ruelle venue te dire bonjour.

Tu dors et le soleil donne sur ta main fermée.

Il y a une enveloppe avec mon écriture sur la table de chevet.

Un mouchoir en boule des pâtes de fruits le radio-réveil et ses chiffres rouges qui lisent midi.

Une pile de magazines miroirs montrant des cyclistes souriant dans des maillots jaunes.

Quand je sors le soleil éclaire aussi ta tête.

Elle est belle là au calme sous les cheveux collés.

Standing beside your bed I've come to say hello.

You're asleep and sun falls on your closed hand.

There's an envelope with my writing on it on the bedside table.

A balled-up handkerchief fruit jellies radio alarm with its red numbers reading noon.

A pile of real life magazines with cyclists smiling in yellow jerseys.

When I go out the sun lights up your head as well.

It's beautiful there in peace under the stuck wet hair.

Du temps du moment chiardemment gone away que nous étions ensemble.

Plus tard j'ai habité des villes.

Et toi passant à Lyon dans ton camion sans mon adresse de bien rangée avec tes disques de stationnement.

C'était au 8, rue Ferrandière je t'y aurais offert un verre.

Ce verre est remis à perpète.

Et tous les autres mortes fêtes.

Au bout d'un fil d'araignée tout rouge et balancé pétale.

Je n'ai rien dans les mains et ma tête est bien vide.

Un bourdon se décoince de tes fleurs puis monte sa vie au ciel.

From the time the moment bloodily *gone away* when we were together.

Later I lived in towns.

And you as you passed through Lyon in your lorry without my carefully put away address with your parking discs.

It was 8, rue Ferrandière, I'd have offered you a drink.

That drink is infinitely postponed.

And all the other parties under the ground.

At the end of a cobweb thread all red and swinging petal.

I've nothing in my hands and my head is really empty.

A bumble-bee frees itself from your flowers then lifts its life into the sky.

Ma grand-mère épluche des fruits au-dessus d'un magazine à sensation.

Le jus dégouline sur le sourire d'un chanteur qu'aiment les vieilles dames.

Elle parle de mon père comme elle connaîtrait bien sa maladie.

Il faut dire qu'elle a longtemps balayé tout un hôpital.

Je ne l'écoute pas je regarde disparaître entièrement le sourire du chanteur le visage du chanteur.

My grandmother's peeling fruit above a gossipy magazine.

The juice runs down on the smile of a singer old ladies love.

She's talking about my father as if she knew his illness well.

Admittedly she swept a whole hospital for years.

I'm not listening to her I'm watching the singer's smile the singer's face completely disappear.

Le voisin matinal est perché sur son toit!

Peut-être est-il en train de prouver son amour à sa femme pas commode.

Peut-être s'est-il sauvé un moment rapproché des nuages feignants.

Il a bon dos tellement humain sans ailes et le vertige.

Il est tout décoiffé il ne va pas tomber pas tomber pas mourir.

Le voilà qui redescend.

En bas madame l'appelle pour ouvrir le salon.

Et c'est une autre histoire.

On trouvait de quoi rire tous deux quand pas les mots.

Mon père et moi d'un rien la coiffure d'une speakerine le chant d'un âne au loin.

Ensemble autour de la table ou sous le ciel changeant, près des portes béates.

Longtemps après que les speakerines ont disparu et les ânes qui chantent de bon cœur.

The morning neighbour's perching on
his roof!

Perhaps he's proving his love to his
demanding wife.

Perhaps he's escaped for a moment
edging closer to the loafing clouds.

He mops up all the blame no wings so
human giddy with the height.

His hair's all ruffled he won't fall not
fall not die.

He's coming down again.

Down there madame is calling him to
open up the shop.

And it's another story.

We'd find something to laugh about the
two of us when words would fail.

My father and me at nothing a
newsreader's hair a donkey's far-off bray.

Together round the table or under the
changing sky, by the why dopen doors.

Long after the newsreaders have gone
and the donkeys braying their hearts out.

Blédine et champe ma régalade alors que ne jase plus rien.

Toi endimanché sans nœud pap dans ton habit de sortir que tu aimais passer inaperçu.

Toute la gaminerie en bouillie la joie en tant de bulles qui pètent.

Suis orpheline et dîne glacé, c'est toi qui dors.

Toi très beau et très droit comme pour une fête longue au moins jusqu'à l'aurore.

Cereal and champers my treat my tipple
now there's no one left to talk.

You in your Sunday best dad but no tie
in your going-out suit that you liked to go
unnoticed.

All the childish mischief boiling up
delight in so many bubbles going pop.

I'm an orphan with my ice-cold dinner,
you're the one asleep.

You very handsome very straight as if
for a long party lasting at least till dawn.

C'est le même vieil oiseau chignole ses ailes cassées.

Tire en l'air et salut ancien au pare-brise où l'étoile rouspète.

Chevaux mal lunés volant vide je passe.

Saute une flaque noire c'est de l'huile à pieds joints.

Pêle-mêle morceaux de choix arbres à cames bielles coulantes.

Sérieux brise-fer en quarantaine sur l'établi marteaux, burins.

Bon ordre des choses à mon père, l'aube redémarre par la fenêtre où l'épave s'ennuie et je passe.

It's the same old crock of a bird its drilling voice its broken wings.

Shoot in the air and ancient greeting to the windscreen where the star is none too pleased.

Ill-mooned horses wheeling empty as I go by.

Jump a black puddle made of oil both feet together.

Choice bits higgledy-piggledy cam-shafts, connecting rods.

Industrial metal-crushers quarantined on the workbench hammers, chisels.

Neatness of my father's things, the dawn starts up again through the window where the pathetic bird gets bored and lets me go.

Les roses les roses je les loue j'en prends que ça comble les trous humaines roses par-dessus tout.

Me pique pour tes yeux tes genoux pour toi voilà des roses partout sans peur des loups sans peur des trous.

Un pot je pose sur ta joue et tourne autour de ce feu fou à ta joue c'est le plus beau rouge.

Oh mon père mon jardin et tout comme bonjour les roses et la boue et le cœur sens dessus dessous humaines roses rouges de tes joues.

Tête-bêche et le cœur qui fait bouh parmi les rosés lourdes comme tout parmi les flammes et les loups vieilles histoires pleines de cailloux.

Ça y est j'ai mis roses partout te laisse mon père faire ton trou dans ma mémoire.

Roses roses I take some full of praises filling the holes above all human roses.

Pricked for your eyes your knees for you there are all over roses no fear of wolves no fear of holes.

I put a pot on your cheek and circle this crazy fire at your cheek it's the loveliest red.

Oh my father my garden everything rosy as pie and mud and the churned-up heart the ruddy human roses of your cheeks.

All head to toe and the heart goes boo among the heavy-headed roses through the flames the wolves old stories full of stones.

That's it I've put my roses everywhere and leave you father in my memory to make your hole.

Je t'écrivais des cartes postales pour tous les jours.

Deux le vendredi donc à cause du dimanche.

Des crocus coloriaient la neige sur la dernière que tu as vue.

Tes doigts devaient trembler à tenir le croissant, et des miettes seront tombées sur la neige.

Mais pour la carte postale du lundi elle est restée dans l'enveloppe dans ta poche dans le cercueil dans le caveau dans la terre, père gigogne.

I'd write you postcards for every day.

So two on Friday because of Sunday.

Crocuses coloured the snow on the last you saw.

Your fingers must have trembled holding the croissant, crumbs must have fallen on snow.

But as for Monday's card it stayed in the envelope in your pocket in the coffin in the vault in the earth, my Russian doll daddy.

Ne plus tenir debout quelquefois tu disais.

Depuis quoi j'ai rêvé que je te relevais que je te relevais et que tu retombais.

Dans la pièce la plus froide tu te serais cassé.

Quand bien même je t'aurais mis debout et tenu aux épaules et parlé à l'oreille apporté des lilas ça n'aurait pas marché.

D'ailleurs je t'ai pleuré dessus ça ne t'a pas remué ni quand j'ai pris ta main dans mes mains bonnes à rien ni rien.

Tu te serais cassé.

Trêve d'éternité.

Dead on my feet you sometimes said.

Since when I've dreamed you were getting up I was getting you up and you were falling back.

In the coldest room you would have got broken.

Even if I could have pulled you to your feet and held you by the shoulder and talked in your ear brought you lilacs it wouldn't have worked.

What's more I cried on you it didn't move you nor when I took your hand in my hands that couldn't do anything or anything.

You would have got broken.

Enough eternity.

Prenant chez mémé café moulu bouillu foutu parlant de ça ta mort bientôt comme on savait même le canari savait tout le monde.

Ma grand-mère donc multipliait ses tupperwares par tes jours qui étaient comptés.

Café bêtu ventru couru j'arrêtai d'en avoir trop bu.

J'aurais pu casser là-dedans le canari les boîtes à conserver les fraises et les fraises que tu aimais.

Parlant de toi et au passé sortant les tasses du buffet.

Et la sueur qui dégoulinait de ton front lui donnait raison.

Café vieillu marc noir repu j'en reprends chez grand-mère rendue toi mort ta mort elle n'en jase plus.

Coffee at gran's her groundup boiledup fuckedup coffee talking about it all your dying soon as we all knew as even the canary knew as everyone.

So my grandmother stockpiled her tupperware in your days that were counted.

Coffees wallowed bellied run away I stopped having drunk too much.

In there I could have smashed the canary containers for freezing strawberries and the strawberries that you loved.

Talking about you as she took the cups from the sideboard and in the past.

And the sweat running off your forehead said she'd got it right.

Oldened coffee blackened dregs full up I'll have another cup worn out turned up at gran's now that you're dead your death her tongue no longer wags.

Juillet à rassembler de grandes fleurs communes par leurs noms.

Trouver les roses plus roses que dans nos souvenirs ma mère et moi.

Je devais encore faire des pointes pour embrasser qui je voulais.

L'acteur hautain à la télévision où je posais un vase.

Bêtes qui montaient des fois des bouquets comme des abeilles comme bonjour à mon père.

Le camion rutilant dort dans les pissenlits, mes frères se parlent doucement dehors avant la nuit.

Leurs mots disent des chiffres ou des étoiles, engueulent un chien et se reprennent.

Ils ont des aigrettes soufflées à leurs cheveux, des traits de cambouis sur la joue et le front.

Lorsqu'ils remontent côte à côte, la route est juste assez large pour eux, et ils se taisent.

July spent bunching together big common flowers by their names.

Finding the roses rosier than we remembered my mother and I.

I still had to stand on tiptoe to kiss who I wanted.

The arrogant actor on the TV where I put a vase.

Bugs that sometimes flew up from the bunches like bees to my father as if to say hello.

The gleaming lorry sleeps in the dandelions, my brothers talk to each other softly outside before it's night.

Their words say stars or numbers, yell at a dog and then go on.

They've got flyaway feathers in their hair, lines of oil across their cheeks and foreheads.

When they come up again side by side the road's just wide enough for them, they don't say a word.

Ta belle tête bandée sous le menton autour de tes joues pourtant pas Pâques papa neuf.

Mon père endurci tes chaussures nouées ensemble tu ne marches plus.

Ta main gauche sur ton cœur ta main droite sur ton foie que ça soit toi le premier vu de mes yeux vu ce reposé.

Ou ton double de cire, plutôt ça d'embrassé.

Avec tes habits pour qu'on puisse pleurer nous tes bon dieu de gamins comme tu grondais, à dire amen sans que ça nous regarde.

Your lovely head in a bandage under the chin around your cheeks and yet not Easter new-laid daddy.

My hardened father boots all tied together you no longer walk.

Your left hand on your heart your right hand on your liver that it should be you the first one seen with my own two eyes this rested man.

Or your double made of wax more like it to my kiss.

In your clothes so we can cry your good God kids as you used to scold us, shouting each other down till kingdom come it's nothing to do with us.

Les mains si froides et ce n'est pas le cœur qui brûle.

Pose une oreille mais elle ne sent rien ni l'autre.

Combien de mouchoirs mettre pour rester un peu encore avec aussi la bouche, les yeux : trouve deux.

Encore un peu une main puis deux nos têtes se cognent même nombre là.

Genoux ensemble.

Pieds joints.

Le cœur est un et ne fait rien.

Ce que devient ton cœur sous les pois de senteur.

Tes mains dures et dorées par les saisons elles changent.

Ton cœur est sous tes mains et toi tout sous les fleurs.

Your hands so cold and it's not your burning heart.

Put my ear but it doesn't feel a thing or the other one.

How many hankies will it take to stay a moment longer with my mouth as well, my eyes: got two.

Just a bit more one hand then two our heads go bump that number is the same.

Knees side by side.

Feet together.

The heart is singular and doesn't do a thing.

What becomes of your heart under the sweet peas.

Your hard hands turning gold with the seasons change.

Your heart is underneath your hands and you completely underneath the flowers.

Il ne t'encolère pas ce gravier gravissime moi m'agace les pieds.

Tu restes bien coiffé, habillé élégant, beau comme prêt à partir.

Ton pantalon très souple, tes tennis tout confort et ton pull préféré.

Moi la jupe qui tombe mal les pompes pleines de gravier m'excuse à peine peignée.

De l'escargot il reste sa coquille, de quoi saisir du ciel avec la pluie venue pour voir dans la coquille.

Ça résiste longtemps sans malice dans le trèfle ou le pissenlit: on regarde le ciel changeant dedans, petit petit.

It doesn't make you cross this gravest of gravels but it irritates my feet.

Your hair's still neatly combed, you're well turned out, and smart as if about to leave.

Your softest trousers, your comfortable trainers and your favourite jersey.

Me in a lumpy skirt my shoes full of gravel sorry hardly combed my hair.

Of the snail there's still its shell, enough to hold some sky with the rain that's come to see inside the shell.

It holds out for ages innocently in the dandelions or clover: you can watch the sky changing inside, little and little.

J'ai mis mes chaussures de marcheuse
celles-là que je t'avais montrées aux
semelles en vieux pneus rechapés.

Pompes pèlerines moi j'ai pèreliné
jusqu'à toi des pétales se collent à leur
cuir comme preuves de ma pensée en
route.

Je sais que tu en as de bonnes toi aussi
à tes pieds tout froids je le sais mieux que
toi et ça t'avance à quoi.

Je voulais te saluer vider le sable éter-
nellement dans mes souliers pour être ta
marchande un peu mais tu as trop fermé
les yeux.

Mon père qu'on opéra mon opéra
mon père fusé dans les nuées.

Père passé sous les azalées dans la
terre jaune et noire et bée.

Ce qu'il devient ce que j'en sais mon
sentiment dans les allées quand le vent
gueule.

I put on my walker's shoes the ones I'd shown you with soles made out of old recycled tyres.

My pilgrimage pumps I've pilgrimed as far as you with petals that stick to their leather like proofs of my thinking on the way.

I know you've got good ones too on your own cold feet I know it better than you and where does that get you.

I wanted to come and see you empty the sand that's for ever filling my shoes be sort of your sandman but you've shut your eyes too tight.

My dad they operated on my operatorio, my dad shot up and melting in the clouds.

Father beneath the azaleas, father goneunder the black and yellow earth that gapes asunder.

What's become of him how should I know my feelings pacing the garden to and fro with the wind howling its head off.

J'amène des fleurs.

Elles retiennent toutes les couleurs elles ont de beaux noms de jeunes filles.

Elles sauront rester plantées là des jours entiers.

Maintenant je m'en vais.

Tu avais de beaux yeux mon père mais j'ai à voir ailleurs.

Tu as mes fleurs j'ai ton sourire on est quitte.

Les yeux tout sales et les doigts froids ce matin j'ai.

Été mal aimable avec la factrice à vélo dans ma chemise de nuit m'a surprise son coup de sonnette.

Nette à présent débarbouillée dans le soleil j'admire les tulipes finissantes et la pivoine en beaux boutons.

Et la pivoine en beaux boutons qui recommence je n'écrirai plus à mon père dessous la terre comme un oignon.

I bring flowers.

They hold on to all the colours they have lovely young girl names.

They'll stay stuck in the ground there waiting for whole days.

Now I'm going.

You had lovely eyes my father but I've other places other things to see.

You've got my flowers I've got your smile we're quits.

Eyes all dirty fingers stiff with cold this morning I've.

Was grumpy with the postwoman on her bike in my nightdress took me by surprise her ring.

Clean now dusted down in the sun admiring the tulips on their way out and the peony's beautiful buds.

And the beautiful budding peony starting again and I won't write any more to my father underneath the earth like an onion.

Ma main là posée sur la table de dehors.

De la même couleur que sa main à mon père.

My hand there resting on the garden
table.

The same colour as the hand that was
my father's.

END-NOTES

Poem 3 (page 22). 'Neige les yeux rouges…'
line 4: literally: "It was when the cows sang that the magpies laughed" – a play on a make of processed cheese (*La Vache qui rit*) and a make of sweet (*La Pie qui chante*).
line 6: literally: "Snow soon goes black like a commonplace, he says."

Poem 17 (page 38) 'Papa dire papa dear…'
line 1, etc: the play between the two languages is untranslatable (*dire* / dear and *rire* / rear in line 3).
line 3 "pas dire": literally "not say", with undertones of "on ne peut pas dire" ('There's no getting away from it').

Poem 19 (page 42) 'Parmi la dînette en morceaux…'
line 4 "dédèle" and line 7 "dédé": Dédé is a shortened form of the father's name André; the little girl wants a nickname that is a feminine version of his.

Poem 27 (page 52) 'Vieux vieux papiers…'
César: the Marseilles-born sculptor César Balaccini, who used scrapyard junk and car compressions as raw material. He died in 1998.

Poems 27 & 54 (pp.52 & 88) 'Vieux vieux papiers…' & 'Le rêve à Kenichie Horie…'
Kenichi Horie: "In 1996, Kenichi Horie (Japan) made the fastest ever crossing of the Pacific in a solar-powered boat when he travelled 10,000 miles from Salinas, Ecuador, to Tokyo, Japan, in 148 days." (*The Guinness Book of World Records*)

Poem 62 (page 100) 'Blédine et champe…'
line 1: "Blédine" is a make of baby-cereal.

BIOGRAPHICAL NOTES

VALERIE ROUZEAU was born in 1967 in Burgundy, France and now lives in a small town near Paris, Saint-Ouen, well-known for its flea-market. She has published a dozen collections of poems, including *Pas revoir* (le dé bleu, 1999), *Va où* (Le Temps qu'il Fait, 2002) and more recently *Apothicaria* (Wigwam, 2007) and *Mange-Matin* (l'idée bleue, 2008) She has also published volumes translated from Sylvia Plath, William Carlos Williams, Ted Hughes and the photographer Duane Michals. She is the editor of a little review of poetry for children (from 5 to 117 years old) called *dans la lune* and lives mainly by her pen through public readings, poetry workshops in schools, radio broadcasts and translation.

SUSAN WICKS, poet and novelist, was born in Kent, England, in 1947. She read French at the Universities of Hull and Sussex, and wrote a D. Phil. thesis on André Gide. She has lived and worked in France, Ireland and America and has taught at the University of Dijon, University College Dublin and the University of Kent.

She is the author of five collections of poetry including *Singing Underwater* (1992), which won the Aldeburgh Poetry Festival Prize, and *The Clever Daughter* (1996), which was short-listed for both the T. S. Eliot and Forward Prizes, and she was included in the Poetry Society's 'New Generation Poets' promotion in 1994. A short memoir, *Driving My Father*, was published in 1995.

She is also the author of two novels, *The Key* (1997), the story of a middle-aged woman haunted by the memory of a former lover, and *Little Thing* (1998), an experimental novel about a young Englishwoman living and teaching in France.

Her most recent book of poems, *De-iced*, came out from Bloodaxe in 2007, and a book of short stories, *Roll Up for the Arabian Derby*, from Bluechrome in 2008.

STEPHEN ROMER was born in Hertfordshire in 1957, and is a lecturer at the University of Tours in France. He has also been Visiting Professor in French at Colgate University, New York. His own poetry collections include *Idols* (1986); *Plato's Ladder* (1992); and *Tribute* (1998). He has translated many French poets, including Philippe Jaccottet, Jean Tardieu, and Jacques Dupin. He has also translated sections from the *Notebooks* of Paul Valéry (2002). His latest collection of poetry is *Yellow Studio* (2008), short-listed for the 2008 T. S. Eliot Prize.

Stephen Romer is also the editor of *20th-Century French Poems* (2002).